Kim Jong-un: The Mysterious and Controversial Life of North Korea's Supreme Leader

By Charles River Editors

About Charles River Editors

Charles River Editors is a boutique digital publishing company, specializing in bringing history back to life with educational and engaging books on a wide range of topics. Keep up to date with our new and free offerings with this 5 second sign up on our weekly mailing list, and visit Our Kindle Author Page to see other recently published Kindle titles.

We make these books for you and always want to know our readers' opinions, so we encourage you to leave reviews and look forward to publishing new and exciting titles each week.

Introduction

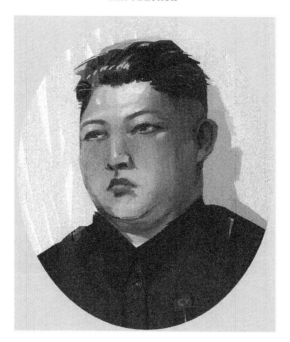

Monico Chavez's sketch of Kim Jong-un

Kim Jong-un

"There is no force in the world that can block the powerful march of our army and people, who are holding high the banner of the suns of great Comrade Kim Il Sung and great Comrade Kim Jong Il and continuing to advance under the leadership of the party and with strong faith in sure victory." – Kim Jong-un

A tyrannical lineage secured by nepotism. An entire nation indoctrinated by chilling, mindboggling propaganda, molded by fear and forced ignorance. Mass purges doled out seemingly on whims, without fair trials. Unparalleled paranoia and cold-blooded assassinations left and right, seemingly around every curve and corner. An impoverished sphere of barren wastelands inhabited by malnourished masses, orbiting a world glittering with the gross opulence and superfluous riches of the elite.

These sound like the elements of a particularly perilous period of autocracy enforced by some mad monarch of a bygone era, or perhaps a generic blurb for a far-fetched thriller set in a dystopian future. Alas, in certain areas of the world, even to this day, these horrifically archaic conditions are anything but fiction. Despite the leaps and bounds in societal progress that most of modern civilization has made, a number of nations have barely budged, powerless to even bend their knees.

While some are merely held back by the looming hurdle of a failing economy, the far less fortunate are impeded by impossibly dense, impenetrable walls on all four corners fencing them in, erected by the dangerously ambitious, self-serving overlords who claimed to have the people's best interests at heart. The Democratic People's Republic of Korea, better known colloquially to the rest of the world simply as North Korea, is infamous for being one of the latter.

To say that the so-called "Supreme Commanders" of North Korea have been sticklers for submission would trivialize the more-than-troubling state of affairs that has plagued this precarious place for decades. The fearsome Kim regime, though relatively fresh in comparison to powerful dynasties that lasted for centuries, has become one of history's most controversial bloodlines, not without cause. This is why Kim Jong-un, the baby-faced 30-something with the bizarre flat-top seated at the throne today, is an object of such fascination. The world watched with bated breath as the keys to the sinking ship was passed down to the young Kim, hoping for the state's long-awaited metamorphosis. It would not take long for these same wishful thinkers to realize that this young man could be far more erratic, blinkered, and inflexible than those came before him.

Kim Jong-un: The Mysterious and Controversial Life of North Korea's Supreme Leader analyzes the known and unknown about one of the most important leaders in the world today. Along with pictures depicting important people, places, and events, you will learn about Kim Jong-un like never before.

Despot in the Making

"Great ideology creates great times." – attributed to Kim Jong-il

"There can be neither today without yesterday, nor tomorrow without today." – attributed to Kim Jong-un

On December 19, 2011, news agencies around the globe hustled to break the shocking news of the death of North Korea's Dear Leader, Kim Jong-il. Many across the world huddled around their screens, big and small, as their local news stations aired the same televised announcement by the Korean Central Broadcasting Committee, the state-owned broadcaster and the only source of media accessible by North Korea's citizens. On these screens was the fabled face of Ri Chun-hee, the head reporter of KCTV. Only, instead of the Barbie-pink *joseon-ot* (the state's version of the traditional Korean dress, the *hanbok)* or brightly-colored '80s style suits Chun-hee was most known for, the visibly grief-stricken woman was dressed in solid black, broken up only by the sliver of white lining her collar. Her drooping eyes were fixed onto the sheets of paper in front of her, which she handled with shaking hands, tears staining her quivering, pasty-white cheeks. "Our great comrade, Kim Jong-il, the General Secretary of the Workers' Party of Korea, the chairman of the DPRK National Defense Commission, and the Supreme Commander of the Korean People's Army, has passed away," Chun-hee announced, lifting her agonized gaze to the camera for the first time. Though dialed down, the fluctuating warble to her voice was still present as she spoke. "He died of a sudden illness on the 17th of December," Chun-hee continued, but not without her voice cracking. "We make this announcement with great sorrow...We took every emergency measure we could, but the Great Leader has passed away."

Kim Jong-il and Vladimir Putin

Based on the statement issued by the state, Kim Jong-il had suffered a fatal heart attack in the private carriage of his train en route to an unspecified destination for one of his "onsite guidance tours." He was 69 years old. Rumors had long swirled about the "immortal" leader's deteriorating health, but news of the ruler's abrupt death was still surprising, and North Korea's neighbors and distant foreign powers alike fretted over who would be handed the reins to this squalid state of 23 million. Furthermore, it had taken North Korean authorities at least two days to issue this statement, a sign many took to indicate a struggle in transition.

Just a few hours later, everyone would have their answer. The mysterious figure at hand was unveiled as none other than Kim Jong-un, the youngest son of the deceased. Though he was no older than 27 or 28 – his identity itself hurtling out of left field only a few months earlier – the statement issued by the Workers' Party marketed him as "the great successor to the revolution" and the "eminent leader of the military and the people," for he was yet "another leader sent from the [sic] heaven." The statement urged its seemingly traumatized citizens to stay strong during this harrowing time, for under the leadership of their new beloved leader, Kim Jong-un, it was their responsibility to "turn sadness into strength and courage, and overcome today's difficulties."

Following this epoch-making declaration, the state broadcasting committee instituted an 11-day mourning period, effective immediately, and scrambled to make arrangements for a funeral service for the ages, scheduled to be held just 9 days later in the North Korean capital of Pyongyang. And so, on December 28, 2011, the streets of Pyongyang – despite being coated with blankets of gray sludge and ice – were packed with hundreds of thousands of North Koreans, pulsing with what can only be described as hysteria as they bade farewell to their fallen Dear Leader.

It was during these baffling, but immaculately choreographed demonstrations that Kim Jong-un made his debut to the North Korean public as the state's next successor. The stout young man, sporting a dark overcoat that did little to hide his portly figure, waddled along slowly next to his father's hearse, a sleek 5th generation Lincoln Continental limo from 1976. Flanked by a motorcade consisting of military trucks and Mercedes-Benz classics, including one with an enormous portrait of a beaming Kim Jong-il mounted on top of it, the hearse rolled forth, followed by a sea of marching soldiers wielding the royal-red and gold flags of the Workers' Party as they trudged across the unforgiving snow. The haunting, hair-raising cries of those lining each side of the 25-mile route drowned out the whistling wind.

The flag of the Workers' Party

These mourners, comprising children to soldiers and senior citizens, male and female, seemed to be beside themselves with despair. They clung on to each other as they wailed, their chests heaving as they gasped desperately for air. The loss of their precious leader was so devastating to some that their knees had buckled, unleashing almost musical sobs as they pounded the icy tarmac with their fists. One soldier interviewed by the state media referenced the gray bullets of snow cascading from the dreary skies as he lamented, "How can the sky not cry? The people...are all crying tears of blood."

If the theatrical display of grief seemed staged to the point of inauthenticity, or at the very least seemed wildly overexaggerated, to those on the outside world, that's because it was most likely just that. Word on the street was that the new man in charge was rounding up those who failed to express sufficient sorrow at his father's death. The guilty were tossed into labor camps, where they were made to spend a minimum of 6 months, some never to be heard from again. Likewise, any insults targeting the new leader were enough to land one behind bars. For these reasons, mourners made sure they were not outperformed by those next to them, amping up the waterworks whenever the camera lenses swiveled in their direction.

The revelation about the staged mourners alone served as a glimpse into the regime of the young Kim, but even then, this was only the tip of the unfathomable iceberg.

Experts launched a series of background checks in the hopes of peeling back the layers of the elusive Kim Jong-un, but doing so was a quest in its own right. Upon the revealing of the new leader, the CIA had only a smattering of information. In fact, the agency only had a single picture to start with, that of a grainy, black-and-white headshot of a chubby 11-year-old boy with a bowl-cut and a cheeky grin. Kim Jong-il had kept his children tucked away from the public eye for years, and it was done so effectively that Kim Jong-un had only been revealed to his soon-to-be subjects about a year before his rise to power.

Even his year of birth continues to be contested. The U.S. Treasury Department lists his date of birth as the 8th of January in 1984, whereas North Korean authorities insist he was born in 1982. Multiple reports suggest that it had been altered to coincide with the birth years of his father and grandfather, born in 1942 and 1912, respectively.

Kim Jong-un was the son of Kim Jong-il and one of his mistresses, Ko Young-Hee, a former opera singer and dancer. Ko Young-Hee was supposedly styling a wedding ring herself when the pair first became acquainted during one of Kim Jong-il's private dance parties in 1972. As the story goes, Kim Jong-il became smitten the moment he laid eyes on her, and he ordered for her to move in to one of his princely villas at once. Whether or not Ko Young-Hee did so of her own volition has died with her, but defectors who were once employed by the pair often spoke about the love and companionship that eventually blossomed between them. "Ko Young-Hee has [Kim Jong-il's] heart," one recounted. "I don't think he has another woman in his heart...She was the only one who could tell him 'no.' I have never seen anyone say no to Kim Jong-il, not even high-ranking officials." The same source went on to describe an intimate scene he stumbled upon, which involved Young-Hee hovering over Kim Jong-il as she trimmed his hair, the pair's eyes glued to one another as they cracked jokes and laughed with another. The scene was said to have been so tender that it prompted the witness to request an equally sensual haircut from his wife later that evening.

Kim Jong-un, the fourth of Kim Jong-il's children, was kept at home with his mother for the bulk of his early childhood. He had an older brother named Jong-Chul, and a younger sister named Yo-Jong, as well as an older half-sister, Sul-Song, and a half-brother, Jong-Nam, born to different mothers. Being the youngest of the Dear Leader's sons, Young-Hee doted on Kim Jong-un, showering him with endless gifts and special attention. A rare photograph that later surfaced showed her lovingly watching over a 5-year-old Kim Jong-un as he practiced his writing, dressed to impress in a spiffy general's jacket tailored to his fitting. Young-Hee saw such promise in her youngest son that she is said to have actively endorsed him as the heir in the years leading up to her death. When she succumbed to complications from breast cancer in 2004, the 20-year-old Kim Jong-un, along with the heartbroken Kim Jong-il, was inconsolable for days.

As common knowledge dictates, the deeper a child is nestled in the lap of luxury, the more challenging it is to foster a sense of empathy and instill in them a healthy worldview. Not only did Kim Jong-un live an absurdly lavish lifestyle, his perception of the real world was further stunted by his limited access to "normal" human interaction. Outside of his siblings and countless servants, the young boy had only ever been around a select few of Kim Jong-il's most trusted officials.

Among the men in Kim Jong-il's inner circle was a Japanese chef known only by his pseudonym, Kenji Fujimoto. Most of what is known about Kim Jong-un's early years was extracted from the tell-all books regarding the Kims' lives that Kenji Fujimoto published when he fled from the state in early 2001. Fujimoto had initially been hired as a private sushi chef to Kim Jong-il and his right-hand men in 1988. He also prepared the lunches of Kim Jong-il's young children, noting that the chunky Kim Jong-un and his father shared a favorite sushi dish, one made out of *toro*, the prized, flavorful fat derived from blue-fin tuna. In time, Fujimoto slithered his way into Kim Jong-il's inner circle, and he was eventually promoted to a senior staff position, which came with a $58,700 USD annual salary and two Mercedes-Benz 500 models religiously polished by his own minions, among other perks.

Fujimoto prepared his young masters' meals for close to two years before Kim Jong-il felt comfortable enough to introduce the chef to his sons. He recalled how Jong-Chul extended his hand without being prompted, gripping his hand with vigor surprising for a 9-year-old. 6-year-old Kim Jong-un, on the other hand, lingered behind his father's legs with a pout on his pudgy face. The boy halfheartedly stretched out a hand only after a subtle nudging from his father, and even then, the scathing scowl he shot at Fujimoto sent a tingle down the chef's spine. The seeds of prejudice appeared to have been planted in Kim Jong-un at an impressionable, young age. "I still cannot forget the look in his eyes," Fujimoto later recalled with a pensive wag of his head. "It seemed to say, 'This is a despicable Japanese.'"

Fujimoto would only succeed in taking apart the first brick from the wall of distrust young Kim Jong-un had built a few days later. Kim Jong-un, who had been gifted a Japanese kite earlier that morning, was throwing something of a tantrum, for his toy refused to take flight. Sensing an opportunity, Fujimoto requested for a few squares of Japanese paper, and, armed with tape and scissors, he proceeded to patch up the holes of the kite. Once it was properly fine-tuned, he stooped down to the ground and handed it back to the still-huffy Kim Jong-un, and with the help of a translator, instructed him to release the kite line. As the kite soared up into the skies, Kim Jong-un bounced up and down with glee, flashing Fujimoto his first smile. It was then, the chef insisted, that Kim Jong-un first "opened his heart" to him.

From that day forward, Fujimoto, under Kim Jong-il's command, doubled as a playmate for his youngest son, and while he grew to love him as one of his own (or so he claimed), he did not shrink back from dishing about the bratty, reckless stunts Kim Jong-un pulled as a child, as well as the maniacal outbursts he was prone to throughout his youth. His behavior was only enabled by the band of servants that bent over backwards to cater to Kim Jong-un's every desire, no matter how ludicrous. They dared not upset their young master, lest they be bussed off to a labor camp or face an even worse fate. They were so eager to please him that when 7-year-old Kim Jong-un demanded to drive one of the officials' new Mercedes, they agreed. Kim Jong-un then hopped onto a booster chair they had installed for him in the driver's seat and clutched the steering wheel. In the passenger's seat, an ashen-faced servant fed him instructions, sweating profusely out of every pore as he struggled to keep the car from swerving without angering the boy. It was here that Kim Jong-un's love for the brand was conceived; he eventually went on to accumulate over 10 Mercedes models, all bulletproof.

Young Kim Jong-un constantly requested the company of Fujimoto on jet-skiing and motorcycling adventures, but he also found in the chef a convenient errand boy. Fujimoto was often sent on intercontinental caviar and cognac runs. As the rest of Kim Jong-il's subjects, struck by one food shortage after another, withered away to skin and bones, Fujimoto was boarding one of the Kims' private jets to Japan for fresh fish, or to Beijing, where he could pick up a dozen Big Macs to satisfy Kim Jong-un's finicky cravings.

Though "no" was a word that had rarely – if ever – graced Kim Jong-un's ears, he, like many teenagers, kept his share of secrets from his father. On top of his eating habits, Kim Jong-un picked up the unhealthy vices of smoking and drinking at just the age of 14. Special edition *Yves Saint Laurent* cigarettes packaged in black-and-gold continue to be his go-to brand, which retails for about $44 per pack. The teenager bribed Fujimoto and other servants to pick up these cigarettes for him, but he often squandered his stash before the next run. He would then bang on Fujimoto's door in the wee hours of the night, begging to bum one from him.

Around the same time, Kim Jong-un began to partake in booze, and he became something of an alcoholic before the age of 18. His tolerance was built on expensive vodka imported from Russia, but Kim Jong-un personally preferred *Cristal* champagne. According to the stories, he could down two $229 bottles of it in one sitting.

Needless to say, his explosive temper was exacerbated by all the alcohol consumption. He left empty bottles littered around the palace like a trail of breadcrumbs. His servants slipped in and dutifully cleaned up after him, knowing all the while to keep their distance.

As all of this would suggest, it did not take long for Kim Jong-un's understanding of money to become irreversibly warped. Aside from the "Olympic-sized" swimming pools, herds of horses, and countless mountains of gifts and entertainment he was exposed to, the teenager owned a pair of super yachts, its multiple decks kitted out with top-of-the-line amenities. His spending sprees snowballed unchecked to such a degree that he reportedly splurged a whopping $716 million on personal expenses in just 2012 alone, more than double the usual $300 million limit set by his predecessors.

Regardless of his hedonistic upbringing, Kim Jong-un, like many boys his age, climbed back into his shell at the presence of the opposite sex. In his late teens, Kim Jong-un became a reluctant attendee of Kim Jong-il's private "pleasure brigade" parties. These brigades, otherwise known as "pleasure troupes," consisted of the most beautiful young women – many of them underage by Western norms – the state had to offer, and they were recruited to perform erotic massages and other sexual favors for Kim Jong-il and his officials. Kim Jong-un was painfully shy around the women, and Fujimoto claimed that he championed monogamy. As such, he regularly turned down the women's advances, which led his concerned father to question his son's sexuality more than once. Fujimoto himself privately questioned Kim Jong-un's sexuality for a time, until the 18 year old admitted to being smitten by one of his father's dancers.

It is easy to be swayed by Fujimoto's stories, as it is the juiciest and most colorfully detailed of all existing accounts on Kim Jong-un's early life. With that said, it must be stressed that Fujimoto's credibility is often called into question. He raked in about $1,000 for every public appearance made in his motherland – not to mention the profits from his books – leading some to speculate that many of these details had either been embellished or fabricated altogether.

There also exists some evidence, in the form of school records, that suggests a portion of Kim Jong-un's teenage years was spent in Switzerland. Kim Jong-un and Jong-Chul, posing as "Pak-Un" and "Pak-Chol," may have been enrolled at either the International School of Berne, or the Liebefeld Steinhölzli Academy, where they studied English and polished up on their French and German on the side. If so, the school staff was clueless about their real identities, and teachers were instead told that the boys were either the sons of a North Korean diplomat or a driver from the embassy. Not one school official ever met the boys' actual parents; North Korean envoys were sent on behalf of their parents, for they supposedly could not speak a lick of English, Swiss, or German.

The classmates of both Pak-Un and Pak-Chol have since come forward to share their schoolyard memories with various news outlets. Pak-Un's schoolmates remembered him as a fairly timid, socially awkward teenager who had been held back two grades upon his arrival due to his lacking language skills. As a result, he found it even more difficult to blend in with his classmates. A photograph from the school yearbook shows a 12-year-old Pak-Un sandwiched between a pair of tall boys in the back row. Clad in a Nike shirt and his eyes in mid-squint under the glare of the sunlight, he looked no different than a typical schoolboy.

When Pak-Un eventually warmed up to his classmates, they soon found that his interests were that of a typical schoolboy. His eyes lit up at the mention of American action movies, especially those starring Jean-Claude Van Damme and Keanu Reeves. But nothing quite compared to his obsession for the NBA, or the sport of basketball in general, which was reflected in his "fantastic collection" of Nike sneakers and the posters of Michael Jordan and other Chicago Bulls superstars that were plastered all over his bedroom walls. Pak-Un was also at his most comfortable on the basketball court, proving to be a relatively gifted player. He might have been heavy-set, but he was two years older than his classmates and thus taller than most of them, which played to his advantage. What was more, his bashfulness in the classroom evaporated on the court, even engaging in good-natured trash talk every so often. "He was a fiercely competitive player, very explosive," Nikola Kovacevic, an ex-classmate, mused. "He was the play-maker. He made things happen."

Be that as it may, another former chum, Marco Imhof, recollected how Pak-Un would storm off the court to throw a fit whenever things failed to go his way. "He hated to lose," said Imhof. "Winning was very important [to him]."

Outside of the campus and the court, Pak-Un spent the rest of his time holed up in his room, which was furnished with the latest gadgets and consoles, as well as a library of the newest games. A few even claim to have been invited to his palatial playroom a handful of times. Apart from the friends he eventually made through basketball, Pak-Un befriended other foreign students, such as Imhof, many of whom hailed from countries that were allegedly "enemies of North Korea." After all, Imhof explained, "Politics was a taboo subject at school...we would argue about [sports], not politics." Imhof went on to add, "[Pak-Un] was funny. Always good for a laugh."

At the end of the day, many have found loose threads and inconsistencies in the statements taken from the Kim brothers' former schoolmates. Even so, in 2012, researchers from the University of Lyon juxtaposed a photograph of the schoolboy from the Liebefeld Steinhölzli Academy with a headshot of Kim Jong-un as an adult, and with the aid of facial recognition software, discovered a 95% match between the two faces. Many believe this is enough evidence to place Kim Jong-un in Switzerland during the early '90s.

Kim Jong-un reportedly returned to North Korea in 2002 and was promptly enrolled at the Kim Il-Sung Military University for the next five years, but dubious observers on the outside world beg to differ. Many suspect his stint in military school to be far shorter, whereas others assert that Kim Jong-un had never experienced a second of training at all. Instead, these skeptics believe that the North Korean government had either inflated or falsified Kim Jong-un's credentials to soothe the public's worries about handing over the state to such young hands. Kim Jong-un would later go on to receive an honorary doctorate from the HELP University in Kuala Lumpur, Malaysia, earning the distinction of being the first foreign leader to acquire such a merit.

An even bigger point of controversy surrounding Kim Jong-un's schooling involves a 24-year-old graduate from Brigham Young University by the name of David Sneddon. Back in August 2004, David, a Mormon missionary and backpacking enthusiast who was fluent in Korean, attempted to cross the cragged terrain of the Tiger Leaping Gorge in China's Yunan Province. In the process, he lost his footing and plummeted to his death. David's body, which was supposedly swallowed up by the raging currents below, has never been found.

In the years that followed, David's family did not believe the official version of events, and in September 2016, a report that surfaced from a South Korean organization that specialized in North Korean kidnappings presented claims that gave weight to their suspicions and rekindled their dwindling hope for the return of their son. David, the organization claimed, had been abducted by state agents at the Chinese border and taken back to Pyongyang, where he was hired as an English tutor for Kim Jong-un and other North Korean officials. In fact, David was more than just safe and sound; the report claimed he was married with two children of his own. His brothers, who had flown to China to search for David themselves, also chanced upon more than one local who recalled spotting a man matching David's description at Tina's Guesthouse, a youth hostel situated on the other end of the gorge. If it was David who these locals had come across, this could only mean that he had made it across, which makes the open-ended case all the more chin-scratching.

It would have made perfect sense for Kim Jong-il's eldest boys, Jong-Nam or Jong-Chul, to follow in their father's footsteps, but why were these sons overlooked? For one, Jong-Nam wrecked his chances when he was apprehended by Japanese authorities for attempting to enter Japan with a forged passport from the Dominican Republic in 2001. When asked why, a sheepish Jong-Nam replied that he wanted nothing more than to experience the marvels of Tokyo's Disneyland for himself.

Jong-Chul was a black sheep of a different breed. He was deemed much too "effeminate" and "girlish" by his father, a sentiment echoed by Fujimoto in his memoirs. Even when Jong-Chul and Kim Jong-un played against each other, Jong-Chul was a "kinder team captain" and a much softer opponent, whereas Kim Jong-un, who was far more aggressive, often taunted rival players. Jong-Chul, who was once photographed with pierced ears and a leather jacket, was also much more Westernized, and he did what he could to avoid politics, opting instead to spend his days in Europe, rocking out in Eric Clapton concerts and partying with his friends.

But in Kim Jong-un, Kim Jong-il saw a version of himself, one even feistier and more headstrong than he was. He made it no secret that he favored his youngest son most out of all his children, often ruffling the hair of his young son as he chuckled, "This boy is like me."

Above all, perhaps the most curious event of all the adventurous episodes of Kim Jong-un's youth was a conversation that allegedly transpired between him and Fujimoto. As the pair sat in Fujimoto's car during a cigarette break late one evening, the 18-year-old broke the silence with a peculiar question that seemed miles outside of his character. "We are here, playing basketball, riding horses, riding jet-skis, having fun together," said Kim Jong-un ruefully. "But what of the lives of the average people?"

Alexander Hagerty, another one of Pak-Un's classmates from his Swiss school days, was another who saw a glimmer of hope in the new state leader. "[His Western education] will make him realize that he has to do something good for his people, for his country, and make a change in terms of past experience, from his knowledge of foreign languages, and the skills he managed to attain from being abroad."

It wouldn't take long for Hagerty, and others like him, to be singing an entirely different tune.

All Hail the Supreme Leader

"Success in the revolution and construction depends on how a party, the General Staff of the revolution, is built, and on how its leadership role is enhanced." – attributed to Kim Jong-un

In late June 2012, the international presses went wild when they unearthed a new photograph of North Korea's new Supreme Leader. The photograph, taken a few weeks earlier, showed Kim Jong-un seated next to an unidentified, attractive young woman. The mysterious maiden, whose round, lightly-rouged face was framed by her neatly-cropped, jet-black hair, wore a dark European suit and dress ensemble that complemented the trademark black overcoat worn by Kim Jong-un. Some were convinced that this was none other than his rarely-photographed younger sister, Yo-Jong, whereas others believed she bore a striking resemblance to Hyon Song-Wol, one of Kim Jong-un's girlfriends. The pair had supposedly sparked a romance shortly after Kim Jong-un's return from Switzerland. Hyon Song-Wol was one of the lead vocalists for the Bochonbo Electronic Orchestra, a North Korean musical troupe that dominated the industry with their "contemporary" renditions of revolutionary anthems and folk songs, the only music allowed in the state. She shot to national fame with her original hit, "Excellent Horse-Like Lady," which was released in 2005. The chart-topper's kitschy music video adorned the screens of North Korean television sets for months. Watery, half-open eyes followed Song-Wol as she pranced about the "sparkling" set of a factory, "distributing bobbins and collecting swatches of cloth" as she caroled her heart out. "Our factory comrades say in jest, why, they tell me I am a virgin on a stallion, but after a full day's work I still have energy left," she sang. "Mounting a stallion my Dear Leader gave me, all my life I will live to uphold his name!"

In spite of Song-Wol's apparent patriotism, Kim Jong-il refused to give his blessings and demanded that the pair be separated at once. Thus, per his wishes, the couple supposedly broke things off in 2006. Not long after, Song-Wol was engaged to another North Korean Army officer. The leaking of the photograph 6 years later, however, triggered a new wave of gossip suggesting that the pair had secretly reunited after Kim Jong-il's death in December of 2011. Footage recovered from the International Women's Day that year further fueled these speculations, for among the dancers of the parade was Song-Wul, with a pronounced baby bump poking out of her *joseon-ot.*

It was only in early July 2012 that North Korean authorities released a press statement to remedy these rumors. The woman in question was not Song-Wol, state officials proclaimed, but Ri Sol-ju, the First Lady of North Korea and wife to Kim Jong-un, as of 2009. It is not clear whether or not the pair had dated beforehand, but South Korean sources suggest that the matchmaking was hastily arranged by Kim Jong-il following a particularly severe stroke in 2008. Like most North Korean figures, not much is known about Ri Sol-ju, and what little information is known about her is obscured by a fog of uncertainty. She was born in Pyongyang to Communist parents – her mother, a doctor, and her father, a scholar – and belonged to the upper echelons of North Korean society. She attended a private school in the capital, where she was classically trained in music and performance arts. Though her story is sometimes depicted as something of a rags-to-riches fairy tale, given the educational privileges and opportunities that she had, the reality is most likely the contrary.

It appeared as if Kim Jong-un had a clear type. Like his ex-girlfriend, Ri Sol-ju was a professional songstress and dancer, and was once a member of a North Korean pop group. On top of her exceptional beauty and effortless feminine grace, which naturally propelled her to the top tier of society, she belonged to an extremely exclusive club of North Koreans who were permitted to travel outside of North Korea. In 2005, 16-year-old Ri Sol-ju embarked on her first trip beyond the border when her cheerleading squad competed at the Asian Athletics Championship in Seoul.

Some experts assert that Ri Sol-ju's pop career prior to 2009 was much too risqué for North Korean standards, which might explain the lack of information regarding this period in her life. According to *Business Insider,* North Korean authorities strove to bury any evidence that so much as hinted at the existence of Ri Sol-ju's pop group, going so far as to enact a state-wide confiscation of all her CDs that caused a "commotion in the markets."

Even with the alleged attempts to control her image, Ri Sol-ju was unlike any other former First Lady. Her sophisticated Western-style suits, designer pumps, and chic accessories made her an instant trendsetter. There was such a demand for her style that a new market for knockoff brands was spawned so North Korean women could adopt Ri Sol-ju's style at a discount.

With that established, the unconscionable prices that was (and continues to be) shelled out to keep the First Lady in vogue was another bone of contention. Critics from beyond the borders have underscored the price tags attached to her ritzy apparel. One of the Christian Dior handbags she was pictured with, for example, retails for about $1,600, which amounts to more than 16 times the monthly salary of a local worker, showing just how gaping the divide between the rich and the poor has become in North Korea.

As of today, Kim Jong-un is believed to have fathered three children with Ri Sol-ju, but there are those who theorize that his first child may have been birthed by a different woman, with some pointing a finger at Song-Wol. When news of Kim Jong-un's firstborn made its way into the grapevines back in 2010, Ri Sol-ju was performing with the Unhasu Orchestra on the same day – a collaboration that was captured on tape – showing no signs of having just given birth. Only the parentage of the second and third children – a daughter, named Kim Ju-Ae, born in 2013, and a third born in February of 2017 – have been confirmed. Though the sexes of Kim Jong-un's first and third children cannot be verified, it is widely believed that the power couple have 3 daughters and are still trying to give birth to a son as a future heir.

Following a string of strokes, Kim Jong-il and his cortège had worked behind the scenes to prepare for the inevitable transition of power, and on September 10, 2010, Kim Jong-il officially appointed 26-year-old Kim Jong-un the new *daejang* of the state, a title on a par with a 4-star general in the U.S. Army. North Koreans – mid-ranking officials and low-level soldiers included – would have been understandably disconcerted by such a decision. Notwithstanding the promotion, at this juncture, the North Korean public had no further information to go on, not even a confirmed portrait of an adult Kim Jong-un. Worse yet, their new *daejang,* though having graduated from the military academy his grandfather allegedly founded (which has still yet to be actually proven), had never set foot on the battlefield, nor has he ever been deployed to a foreign military base. Even more troubling tidings came the next day, when it was announced that Kim Jong-un had been named the vice chairman of the Central Military Commission, the body responsible for managing the Korean People's Army and strategizing for future military campaigns. That same day, he was elevated to Chairman of the Central Committee of the Workers' Party. How was he in any way equipped to handle 1.2 million soldiers, the 4th largest army in the world, let alone run the entire state?

The final phase of the transition took shape on October 10, 2010, which marked the 65th anniversary of the founding of the Communist Workers' Party. To celebrate the milestone, Western media outlets and their news crews were invited to the festivities by the normally reticent North Korean authorities for the very first time. Unsurprisingly, every organization that received the invite wasted no time packing up their equipment and jetting off to Pyongyang, heading for the Kim Il-sung Square.

The official portrait of Kim Il-sung

Stealing the spotlight from the sickly, smartly-dressed Kim Jong-il was his guest of honor, Kim Jong-un, who made his first public appearance. Forgoing the traditional *daejang* uniform, the heavyset young man, dressed in his usual crisp black suit, admired the impeccably synchronized routines of the "goose-stepping troops" and other performances from the balcony above. He remained fairly quiet throughout the festivities, speaking only when spoken to and rather rigidly joining his hands together only when those next to him began to clap. The spectacular celebration, which was heavily seasoned with military themes and weapon-parading, not only served to blow foreign spectators and enemies out of the water, it was a sign that Kim Jong-il's "*songun*," or "military-first" policy, was a legacy that his son fully intended to uphold. As a quote later attributed to Kim Jong-un put it, "The people's army should always maintain a highly agitated state and be equipped with full fighting readiness so as to smash the enemies with a single stroke if they make the slightest move and achieve the historic cause of the fatherland's reunification."

On January 9, 2012, approximately three weeks after Kim Jong-un's rise to power, the Korean People's Army was summoned to the Kumsusan Palace of the Sun to pledge their lifelong loyalty to the new Supreme Leader in the form of a rally. Among the songs played was one entitled "Footsteps," a rousing symphonic instrumental that had been arranged and consecrated to the young leader three years prior, but the track played at this rally featured fresh stanzas of equally spirited lyrics. "Tramp, tramp, tramp, the footsteps of our General Kim, spreading the spirit of February," the soldiers belted. "Footsteps, footsteps, spreading out further the sound of a brilliant future ahead. Tramp, tramp, tramp, ah, footsteps."

Three months later, on the 15th of April, Kim Jong-un attended the 100th birthday celebration of his grandfather, aptly held at the Kim Il-sung Square, where he would deliver his first public speech. Following a riveting tribute to the grand patriarch of the state, Kim Jong-un segued into a tirade concerning his martial objectives. He made it clear that his "first, second, and third priorities" were to reinforce the KPA at once, and he boasted not only of the abilities of its high-caliber marksmen and troops but the North Korean's alleged supremacy in military technology, for the sphere was "no longer monopolized by imperialists." Most alarming of all was his commitment to light a fire under the state's highly controversial nuclear and missile programs.

The speech, which was greeted by the deafening cheers of his audience, was topped off by the grandest exhibition of North Korean weaponry thus far. Claiming center stage during the military parade was a glinting long-range missile. Though those on the outside were uncertain as to whether or not the missile was the real deal, the display understandably caused great consternation. Moreover, a few days earlier, North Korea had launched a 30-m Unha-3 rocket in the direction of Japan and the Philippines. Fortunately, following a flight time of just under a minute, the rocket crumbled into 20 pieces and plopped into the sea without further incident. North Korea was chastised for breaking the agreement that forbade all nations from conducting long-range missile experiments, but state authorities brushed it off as nothing more than a failed attempt at launching a satellite into orbit to commemorate the 100th anniversary of Kim Il-sung.

Whatever the case, North Korea was certainly undaunted and undeterred by the failure, a reality that has been increasingly unnerving. Having tangoed with his fair share of North Korean officials himself, Victor Cha, once employed by the Bush administration as an international mediator, issued a warning about the impending dark days of the state: "It is clear that this young man is moving to consolidate his leadership in a very aggressive manner with these displays of strength."

Though Kim Jong-un moved to aggrandize his father's militaristic policies, his speech itself showed a clear deviation from the norm. Kim Jong-il, described by journalists and chroniclers alike as "reclusive," had never given a public speech to the North Korean masses. Most locals did not even have an inkling as to what his voice sounded like until 1992, when a quick cutaway showed Kim Jong-il roaring into a microphone amid animated applause: "Glory to the heroic soldiers of the People's Army!"

During the first week of July 2012, shortly before the confirmation of Kim Jong-un and Ri Sol-ju's wedlock, the Supreme Commander was presented with yet another anthem penned just for him. Inspired by his fiery public address, "Onwards Toward the Final Victory," as it was christened, was lifted from the closing words of his speech. When critics branded the anthem as blatant propaganda, Hong Kwang-Sun, who was appointed the DPRK's Minister of Culture that year, defiantly (and rather poetically) responded, "The song is just a powerful trumpet call of the revolution encouraging the army and the people in the drive to build a thriving nation, as well as a stirring drumbeat of victory."

Despite the state's rebuttals, experts are positive that the anthem was only one aspect of a multi-step "propaganda drive" that aimed to polish up the young leader's image. Not only were the score and lyrics printed in the national newspaper, the *Rodong Sinmun*, so that citizens could commit its words to their memories, the song and music video continued to be played on loop on North Korean radios and televisions at least three times a day. While those peeping in from the outside world objected to the tactics, North Korean authorities firmly denied allegations of propaganda. The KCNA insisted, "The song hardens the will of the Korean army and people to devote their all to the prosperity of the country with high national pride."

Yo-Jong served as a public relations manager of sorts for her older brother, and she was entrusted with administering the propaganda drive, as well as developing what historians call a "personality cult." North Koreans were not just expected to adhere to a savagely strict way of life, they were now to adhere to a "manual of idolization" compiled by Yo-Jong and her team, which included a detailed schedule of worship. Even more discomfiting was the unnecessary pomp and pizzazz that quickly followed suit, which only showed the lengths authorities were willing to reach just to maintain an untarnished image of their untouchable leader. For example, reels of postage stamps were retired and replaced with ones that featured the face of the Supreme Commander. In February of 2016, an all-girl singing group founded by Kim Jong-un himself, *Moranbong*, unleashed a new patriotic single, "We Call Him Father," that would take the state by storm. His rumored ex-girlfriend, Song-Wol, is also thought to have been part of the troupe. In October of the same year, a rambling documentary produced and edited by North Korean officials was released to the masses, and later that year, the DPRK committee authorized the construction of a mighty monument to be chiseled in Kim Jong-un's likeness, scheduled to be unveiled in late 2017. It was to be erected by the lake crowning Mount Paektu, which shares a border with China. A series of life-sized mosaic murals to be installed in every province is also currently in the works.

Considering these conditions, it is impossible to escape the propaganda propagated by the regime. The Kim dynasty's faces are the first ones that North Koreans see in the morning, for every citizen was required by law to display their portraits in their bedrooms, sitting rooms, or wherever else it can best be appreciated by the household. On their way to work, be it in the city or province, citizens were accosted by Kim Jong-un's thunderous speeches, which blared from the speakers of the military trucks making their rounds. One such speech, which revolved around a promise for a "bright economic future," was put on loop for three straight months.

As might be expected, these propaganda campaigns have served to undermine morale, not elevate it. This is especially evidenced by footage that has recently emerged of a group of North Korean government officials on their lunch break. Oblivious to the live camera stowed under the table, they took turns airing their grievances, showing just how little faith they had in their leader behind shut doors. "He shouldn't be there," groaned one official. "He can't do anything. He's too young, you know? No matter how hard he tries, even if it kills him, he's hopeless."

A Nation "Renewed"

"Patriotism is not an abstract concept. It begins from one's own home. It buds out from the love for one's parents, spouses and children, the love for one's own home, village and workplace, and further develops into the love for one's own country and fellow people." – Kim Jong-un

It appears that against all odds – namely, the continuous threats of sanctions and increased isolation from major foreign powers – the North Korean economy began to gain some traction in the past few years. As a result, the state's ego continued to swell, so much so that it severed ties unflinchingly and moved forward with their nuclear and missile programs, with or without the help of what few allies they had left.

As much as the outside world enjoys railing against Kim Jong-un, he is said to have been the first in the dynasty to introduce a rehabilitation program geared towards the marketplace. In 2013, the Supreme Commander assured his subjects that his party would tackle and conquer the dilemma of the failing industries. These economic reforms have since succeeded in breeding a small, but gradually growing class of entrepreneurs and traders, their rights protected by the regime's most eminent officials. Though the overwhelming majority of the North Korean population continues to suffer abject poverty, the visibly climbing statistics, no matter how trivial, cannot be ignored. Since Kim Jong-un's rise to power, the state has experienced an annual growth rate between 1 to 5 percent. While this does not seem like much of a growth spurt, experts say it holds a candle to economies that have not been stifled by sanctions. By the end of 2013, the government-approved fields of industry had doubled to about 440, and approximately 1.1 million (a number that has most likely spiked since then) of its 25 million residents had been promoted to a post of manager or retailer in the new markets, showing some semblance of improvement in the quality of life – at least for the fractional middle class. The state capital saw a burst in new construction and renovation projects, and it experienced most of the boom in terms of economic activity. To put it in perspective, what used to be the bleak and barren streets of Pyongyang now teemed with enough cars – albeit mostly old-fashioned, outdated models – that a portion of the population's enterprising minds could make a business out of washing them.

Meanwhile, the state's black markets were simultaneously thriving, perhaps even more so. Many of the unemployed have taken it upon themselves to churn out their own bread and butter – in some cases, literally – from their homes. Other self-made entrepreneurs peddled homemade clothes, shoes, pickled treats, and more from the trunks of their cars. Every 10 days or so, unregistered farmers cropped up on a street corner with wagons of homegrown fruits and vegetables. Smugglers bearing thumb drives chock-full of Western movies and music files, and other contraband snuck in through the Chinese border, stationed themselves in secure spots. Street-hawking was extraordinarily risky, but its sweet profits kept the industry very much alive. Economists estimate that up to 40% of North Koreans engage in some sort of black market activity. Veteran black market barons memorized the schedules of the local patrol force, and knew to skedaddle just in the nick of time.

The North Korean government is fully aware of the underground world of commerce, but seeing as how it is most likely the raft keeping the economy afloat, they have come to condone it. As such, influential North Koreans cushioned by a web of political connections hastened to take advantage of the government's slackened grip, creating sizable private companies of their own. For these reasons, there now exists a number of privately-owned transport companies, oil refineries, and mines.

North Korean women, particularly the affluent ladies from Pyongyang and other larger cities, embraced the changing climate, with their presence in the workforce doubling. Not only did they become the target market for luxury brands, they became the most frequent patrons of upscale restaurants. Pyongyang became known for its diverse selection of cuisine, once available only to foreigners and society's elites. Restaurants and bistros of varying sizes offered exotic Chinese cuisine, imported Japanese sushi, deluxe Italian dishes, and other international delights. There even exists a small village of micro-breweries –requested by noted booze connoisseur Kim Jong-un himself – near the Juche Tower, which carried colorful menus of craft beers from Europe. A full meal with the works in one of these exclusive eateries cost anywhere between $15-$25, which amounts to about a week's worth of pay, but this did nothing to stop winding queues from forming outside of their doors.

Taking a page from the Communist Chinese in the late 1970s, Kim Jong-un set out to revamp the agricultural industries. Tillable plots of land owned by the state were divvied up and apportioned to individual farming households. These farmers agreed to cultivate and work on the land in exchange for 30-70% of the harvests, depending on the stipulations of the agreement. Something about this system must have clicked, for North Korea is closer than it has ever been to being able to support itself in terms of food production.

Kim Jong-un has also directed some of his focus on enhancing the culture of the North Korean youth, as well as the budding middle class. In recent years, the Supreme Commander has commissioned a chain of multi-level department stores, theme parks, and other venues for entertainment to be built in the next decade. The pinnacle of these campaigns came in April 2017, when a grinning Kim Jong-un proudly clipped the ceremonial ribbon with his shiny shears to celebrate the opening of Ryomong Street. The swanky new block, designed by the ambitious young leader himself, was outfitted with a series of spanking-new shops, pharmacies, restaurants, and skyscraping flats.

The improved quality control for the food of the upper classes is another rare rose that has sprouted from Kim Jong-un's thorny regime. Sources say that Kim Jong-un is more than just a picky and irresponsible eater; from outward appearances, it seems that he clearly has no issues with caloric intake, but he is particularly paranoid about the source of his food. Every last thing on his plate, down to the garnishes, would have passed several food safety tests, some so elaborate they entailed the use of microscopes.

All the fresh fruit and greens consumed by the Kim dynasty and North Korean patricians were derived from the June 17 Farm, located in the Yongsong district of Pyongyang. The June 17 Farm, which was actually a cluster of greenhouses founded by Kim Jong-un's father, were staffed with single, 20-something North Koreans that hailed from educated, respectable backgrounds. Almost all graduated with honors, bearing science-related degrees from Kim Il-sung University, the Pyongyang University of Science and Technology, and other prestigious institutions, which they relied on to eliminate the "germs, toxins, and health hazards" from their crops. These greenhouses yielded the state's finest, and therefore most precious, fruits and vegetables, meaning that they came with extortionate price tags and could only be afforded by the richest members of society.

In the mid 2010s, wealthy North Koreans were also granted access to a watered-down version of the Internet for the very first time, a restricted cyberspace dubbed the "*Kwangmyong*," or "Bright." Its purpose was not to serve as a medium for entertainment and overseas communication, but rather function as a mode to broadcast pre-approved messages and information, as well as a line of communication that linked the government to universities and local industries. As of today, only an estimated 1,024 Internet Protocol addresses have been registered in the state, an absurdly small number given North Korea's 25 million residents.

An even smaller portion is allowed unfettered and unfiltered access to the Internet as it is seen by the rest of the world. The limited list of those allowed to log on to the World Wide Web, apart from Kim and his entourage, included high-level bureaucrats, propagandists, researchers, and hackers. Even then, all incoming and outgoing emails and correspondences, downloads, the dirty details of one's browser history, and so forth, are strictly monitored by government officials.

Smartphones have also recently been making an appearance in well-to-do North Korean communities. While most of these models can be synced to the *Kwangmyong*, state-issued smart phones were only capable of making domestic calls. That said, like any smartphone, these could be jail-broken to make and receive international calls for a fee.

Advancements in their nuclear and missile programs aside, the North Korean government, under the guidance of Kim Jong-un, has also bragged about a slew of scientific breakthroughs. In June 2016, news of the Supreme Commander's history-making innovation reached viral fame overnight, one that was guaranteed to forever change the world of medicine. According to authorities, a team of North Korean scientists had cooked up a "wonder drug" that could cure AIDS, Ebola, and various strains of cancer in one go. The miracle cure, which was named the "Kumdang-2," came in the form of an injectable liquid containing a ginseng extract and an assortment of other undisclosed ingredients. Of course, experts believe no such drug exists, and this is only one of the countless far-fetched claims promulgated by Kim Jong-un and his officials, which many believe to be a tactic designed merely to throw enemy powers off their game. The same regime has also claimed that Kim Jong-il, the inventor of the hamburger, was so flawless an entity that there was never a need for him to use a toilet.

As Kim Jong-un and his men worked towards bettering the lives of the elite, the Supreme Commander thought it only befitting to continue the stupendously spendthrift lifestyle he had grown accustomed to. Naturally, with an estimated personal net worth of about $5 billion, it was difficult to run out of dough to spend. Of the $716 million he coughed up in 2012, $37 million went to electronic gizmos, about $8.2 million was spent to luxury watches, another $1 million went to alcohol, and the rest covered his breathtaking dining habits and entertainment expenses. Some are convinced that the national treasury and his personal bank account are one and the same, but others, including CNN, are positive that he cashes in on black market profits, including drug and weapons sales, cash counterfeiting, and hacking banks. Adding to his fantastic fleets of designer cars and his wardrobe, outsiders have repeatedly accused him of going under the knife and tweaking his facial features in an effort to bear a greater resemblance to his grandfather. It did not take long for enraged North Korean officials to stuff a cork in these rumors, writing them off as nothing more than "sordid hackwork by the rubbish media," and a "false report" that the North Korean people "refused to tolerate." All the drama aside, whether or not Kim Jong-un had any work done is still up for debate, but visual evidence shows that the young Kim had, at the very least, inherited his grandfather's mannerisms and adopted his hairstyle.

Kim Jong-un has a variety of magnificent villas and posh palaces at his disposal, but most of his time is spent in Residence No. 55, better known to the public as the "Ryongsong Residence." The colossal compound, which sits in Northern Pyongyang, is tricked out with a plethora of flamboyant facilities, including an underground bunker well-stocked with provisions and encased in impenetrable lead to keep Kim Jong-un and his family safe in the event of a nuclear war or enemy invasion. Bands of armed guards are posted around various areas of the presidential palace for good measure, and to top it all off, the compound was bordered by an electric fence, and a sequence of security checkpoints peppered with mine fields. Those privileged enough to have entered its main structure marveled at its exquisite cream motif, velvety, carpeted floors, glittering chandeliers, and a handsome collection of furniture and artwork. The palace was also decked out with vibrant gardens and sparkling bodies of man-made lakes, as well as various amenities dedicated to leisure, such as a movie theater with a maximum seating capacity of about 1,000 for Kim Jong-un to enjoy private screenings of his favorite action flicks. The Ryongsong Residence also came with five aircraft runways and its own train station, as well as a maze of tunnels that connected it to other presidential residences.

The only outsiders to ever experience Kim Jong-un's lavish, party-happy ways firsthand paint an even more elaborate picture of the Supreme Commander's decadent lifestyle. Contrary to what one might assume, these outsiders were not politicians or bureaucrats, nor were they even related to one. Though these unlikely visitors were complete aliens to the world of politics, they had everything to do with Kim Jong-un's biggest passion: basketball. In 2013, millions scratched their heads when the famous NBA player Dennis Rodman, along with Harlem Globetrotter legends Alex Weekes, Anthony Blakes, and Will Bullard, accepted a remarkably rare invitation to visit the state as the Supreme Commander's VIP guests. Journalists and a small film crew from Vice Media were also permitted to tag along – another anomaly – so that they could obtain footage for a documentary about the events. To this day, Dennis Rodman, who has since found an "eternal friend" in Kim Jong-un, holds the distinction of being the only American to ever interact with the Supreme Commander at such an intimate level. Rodman subsequently explained how he had been given the "seven-star" treatment. The pair shot hoops and watched multiple games from the luxurious comfort of Kim Jong-un's skybox. They then cruised off to one of Kim Jong-un's private resort islands via the leader's $7 million yacht, smoking cigars, feasting on plates of delectable dishes, and popping bottles that cost more than five figures along the way. The island also featured its own entertainment complexes, from roller-coasters and water parks to even more basketball courts and football fields. Not too far off was a "world class" ski resort-slash-paradise that cost about $27.7 million in construction fees, packed with "multi-level ski runs" that stretched 70 miles long, as well as brand-new cable cars, a hotel, and a helipad. "It's like going to Hawaii or Ibiza, but he's the only one that lives there," Rodman said. "He's got 50 to 60 people around him all the time – just normal people, drinking cocktails and laughing the whole time...If you drink a bottle of tequila, it's the best tequila. Everything you want, he has the best."

Given all these tales, tall or otherwise, Kim Jong-un has always been an easy target for caricature. The man also harbored pettiness on a whole other level – in 2016, the Supreme Commander added Christmas to the state's seemingly boundless list of illegalities, ordering his subjects to pay homage to his paternal grandmother, who was born on Christmas Eve, instead. He has even created a new time zone – now 30 minutes behind South Korea and Japan – so as not to coincide with the enemy powers.

The majority of his edicts being as outlandish as they are to the outside world, Kim Jong-un is a perfect magnet for comedy and satire. But while Kim Jong-un might seem more liberal in many ways when compared to his predecessors, his sense of humor has proven to be as fragile as it is limited. The 2014 movie *The Interview,* starring Randall Park, Seth Rogen, and James Franco, is a case in point. The film, which was centered on two zany journalists who embark on a mission to kill Kim Jong-un, was already a sensitive subject by politically correct Western standards, and as expected, North Korea was anything but amused. In fact, officials from Pyongyang equated its release to an "act of war," one that would be met with ruthless retaliation.

Unabashed by the state's threats, the film's producers staunchly refused to back down. A few days later, a hackers' collective that branded themselves the "Guardians of Peace" infiltrated Sony Pictures and proceeded to publish chains of confidential company emails, personal addresses and details swiped from employee files, and raw copies of films scheduled to be released later that year. Attached was a warning that read, "We will clearly show it to you at the very time and places *The Interview* be shown, including the premiere, how bitter fate those who seek fun in terror should be doomed to." Security teams later confirmed that the hackers bore definite ties to North Korea. For security reasons, Sony Pictures made the widely unpopular decision to yank the film from its theaters, which had previously been on track to premiere on the 25th of December. In the end, thanks to all the publicity, *The Interview* became both the highest-selling and most pirated movie on Christmas Day that year, reeling in over 750,000 downloads in just the first 20 hours upon its release.

The Ugly Truth

"Should the enemy dare to invade our country, annihilate them to the last man so that none of them will survive to sign the instrument of surrender!" – A slogan from a North Korean propaganda poster published in 2015

Millions around the world slapped their knees at Randall Park's portrayal of the Supreme Commander – an egotistical, violent, Katy-Perry-loving man-child that was ultimately a softie at heart – but the appalling reality behind Kim's regime is no laughing matter.

When pictures of a giddy Kim Jong-un striking various poses next to his tanks and missiles began to circulate, it was met with scorn and ridicule by the rest of the world. Recently, however, this laughter has ebbed, for more and more experts now believe that out of all his preposterous claims, military bluster may very well be the one thing he isn't joking about. This thought becomes even more dismaying considering the following excerpt from one of his 2013 speeches: "Nuclear weapons guarantee peace, economic prosperity, and people's happy life."

While so much else about the hermit kingdom remains unclear even to the world's foremost intelligence agencies, the history of North Korea's nuclear program is so extensive that analysts have discovered a clear pattern in the North Koreans' modus operandi. They are found to be most hostile when faced with resistance via threats of sanction, increased isolation, or retaliation. These scare tactics, labeled "escalatory moves," include minor threats, such as issuing public warnings, or detonating prototype models of their atomic explosives in their backyards. Further into the spectrum were clear-cut threats that targeted specific countries by name. They have also begun to push limits by launching missiles towards sparsely populated areas, but for now, the North Koreans have adhered to regions that would cause the most minimal collateral damage.

The North Korean government is also currently in the process of developing the "ideal" nuclear weapon. The perfect specimen, say North Korean scholars, is a "miniaturized" missile condensed with a blast of 15 kilotons. Scientists strove to find a way to downsize these missiles and make them more lightweight so that they could reach their destinations with more ease, all the while retaining every last drop of its explosive impact.

Atomic, hydrogen, and neutron bombs are three types of explosives that are believed to be in production, but the extent of their development is still very much muddied. North Korean missiles are further categorized into 3 classes. First, there are the "strategic nuclear weapons," which are essentially heavy-duty bombs that are designed to destroy major industrial centers, as well as small cities. Next are what North Korean scientists call "tactical nuclear weapons," which are explosives that are specially engineered to blow up enemy troops and squadrons, as well as their tanks, warships, and army bases. Then, there are "battlefield nuclear weapons," capable of "medium-range delivery," equipped to wipe out any targets on the "tactical battlefront."

Kim Jong-un knows full well that he has gone beyond playing with fire at this point, indicating that he is both more tenacious and obstinate than his predecessors, and from the looks of it, he does not seem at all anxious about being burned. "If you were the head of a small, isolated, poor country surrounded by potentially hostile military powers, you'd be looking for some way to ensure your own destiny, too," Jon Wolfsthal, a former member of President Barack Obama's National Security Council, explained, potentially shedding some light on the logic behind Kim Jong-un's power tactics. Kim hasn't been shy about saying much the same thing. "The days are gone forever when our enemies could blackmail us with nuclear bombs."

North Korean threats have only seemed to be gaining momentum over the last few years. More precisely, it has continued to single out the United States, its arch-nemesis. In March of 2015, cages around the world were rattled when the authoritarian state released warmongering propaganda disguised as a documentary, one with a message even more abnormally aggressive than usual. "If the American imperialists provoke us a bit, we will not hesitate to slap them with a preemptive nuclear strike. The United States must choose! It's up to you whether the nation called the United States exists on this planet or not." The malicious message was superimposed on a computer-animated missile homing in on Washington.

Kim Jong-un has also begun to toy with other major foreign powers, both near and far, escalating animosity in every direction. North Korea continues to vilify those who make threats against the state, and damns anyone who dares to speak ill of their heavenly leader. In another one of his recent highly-charged speeches, the Supreme Commander ordered his troops to seize all enemies and toss them into a boiling "cauldron," and as they thrashed and flailed in the bubbling water, to shatter their waists and slice open their windpipes.

Another dreadfully unfunny reality about Kim Jong-un's perplexing and petrifying regime are the nightmarish conditions and deplorable quality of life the rest of his subjects are forced to endure. He might have enriched the lives of the richest segment of society, but every other North Korean, owing to the state's paradoxical "planned economy," has been left to fend for themselves. Most find it difficult to adjust from a system that has been drilled into the norm for generations. Just a few decades ago, almost all North Koreans were employed in either state-owned farms or enterprises. For their work, they were compensated with meager salaries, as well as ration coupons that could be swapped for groceries and other essentials in state supermarkets.

Under Kim Jong-il, the system began its phasing out in the late 1990s. Displaced workers and laborers failed to move with the shift in the national industries, and as such, the average state worker is left with no choice but to scrape by on about a dollar a month. "If you are an ordinary North Korean today, and if you don't make money through markets, you are likely to die of hunger," claimed Kim Nal-Chol, a defector from the town of Hoeryong. "It's that simple."

In 2016, the World Food Programme discovered that up to 70% of the 25.1 million North Koreans – 1.3 million of them being children under the age of 5 – suffered from serious "food insecurity." In effect, chronic malnutrition continues to be rampant. The report attached to the findings elaborated, "10.5 million people, or 41 % of the total population, are undernourished." Furthermore, the state's residents face a dire lack of "basic healthcare and sanitation." The lack of clean drinking water and general hygiene continues to wreak havoc upon the North Korean poor, and can be blamed for the pneumonia and diarrhea-related illnesses – the leading causes of death for toddlers and young children – that persistently plague the nation.

To make matters worse, there are accusations of Kim Jong-un deliberately contributing to the starving of the already famished population in an effort to better finance his nuclear campaigns. To begin with, critics have repeatedly castigated Kim Jong-un for his obsessive nuclear experiments, which seem to be spewing more and more updates by the week. Such a move, the critics insist, show proof that the Supreme Commander values a "robust military budget" more than finding a solution to the nation's pressing poverty problem. In conjunction with that, reports show that the state's rations of grains and starches have diminished from about 380 grams to 300 grams of food a day, a drop of approximately 26.6%. Put simply, the poor receive less than a pound of food a day, and these are the more "fortunate" of the plebeian class, for they were at the very least entitled to rations from the state.

Disturbing footage filmed by undercover journalists, which has continued to make its rounds over the years, captures only a peep of the depressing conditions of North Korea's impoverished provinces, which are overflowing with homeless people, most of them orphans. One clip showed a pack of gaunt and frail-looking children rummaging through dumpsters, foraging for their first meal of the day. Another showed a circle of shivering orphans snuggling against one another as they feebly rubbed their hands together over a flickering fire, trying to stay warm during the frigid North Korean winter.

It is easy to mock and criticize Kim Jong-un outside of North Korea, but things couldn't be more different for those trapped there, for they seem to be faced with either a lifetime of excruciating hard labor or instant death for the most trifling misdemeanors. If anything, it seems impossible to adhere to the state's impractical standards. In late August 2013, multiple news agencies reported that all 13 members of Kim Jong-un's beloved girl band, *Moranbong*, had been executed by firing squad for the crime of "violating laws against pornography." His former flame, Song-Wol, was the first name on the list.

Rumor had it that a few weeks earlier, a strange video had been uploaded to *Youku*, a Chinese video platform, which some North Koreans proceeded to share amongst themselves until it caught the eye of bored journalists looking to conquer a slow news day. North Korean officials were mortified when they caught wind of the video, immediately denouncing it as "pornography." A few days later, Kim Jong-un had callously ordered the brutal murder of all those involved in the video to punish them for dishonoring the great state. What was the "pornographic" video in question? It was simply the girl band, dressed in spangled leotards and quirky red hats, swaying to Elvis Presley's "Aloha Oe," a video that was mildly titillating at best. Adding to the confusion, in May 2014, Song-Wol made a rare appearance on television, clearly alive and well, to lay the rumors of her death to rest.

That episode was yet another example of how difficult it is to separate fact and fiction when it comes to North Korea, but while her case has been retired, experts believe that many of these kinds of stories are far from fake news. In December of that same year, verified reports confirmed the demise of Kim Jong-un's uncle, Jang Song-Thaek, once considered an untouchable figure in the seamy world of North Korean politics. In a move that caught even the most hardened political analysts by surprise, Song-Thaek, branded a "traitor for all ages" by his nephew, was accused of plotting a coup. Within a matter of weeks, he had been sentenced to death. The state media continued to drag his name through the mud, citing a lengthy list of additional crimes he had been found guilty of, including "pursuing a decadent capitalist lifestyle," embezzling $3.9 million in state funds, and the illegal distribution of pornography.

In a perverse sense, Jang Song-Thaek's death was proof that there exists some form of fairness within the world of Kim Jong-un, no matter how twisted. Government officials and state employees might be entitled to the dream life most North Koreans yearn for, but if they rub Kim Jong-un the wrong way, it all can vanish with just a snap of a finger. One unfortunate soul to cross the Supreme Commander beyond the point of return is an unnamed owner of a state greenhouse that failed to meet his standards. Kim Jong-un has also reportedly executed an entire panel of engineers that were responsible for a faulty tower that collapsed, killing more than 100 of its inhabitants.

In addition to cooking up charges against people, it seems Kim Jong-un has also gotten creative with the actual executions. The most notorious example to date came with the alleged execution of a defense minister, Hyon Yong-chol, who was officially sentenced to death for treasonous activities. Rumor had it that he had enraged Kim by falling asleep during a meeting, and as a result, he was shot by a four-barreled anti-aircraft artillery piece.

The boldest of all of Kim Jong-un's murderous schemes to date came on the 13th of February, 2017, and it was a scheme so convoluted and extreme that it would put most Hollywood spy flicks to shame. That morning, Kim Jong-Nam, the Supreme Leader's older half-brother, navigated his way through the bustle of the Kuala Lumpur International Airport, slamming on the gas so as not to miss his 10:00 a.m. flight to Chinese Macau. But as he fumbled with his belongings by the check-in counters, a pair of young women who took note of his distraction sidled up to him from behind. Before he could react, one of the women seized him from behind, while the other lunged forth and clamped a moist handkerchief onto his face, pressing it firmly over his nose and mouth until he finally broke free.

The peculiar interaction was so subtle that no one but the security cameras had taken a second glance at them. As the women shuffled off in the opposite direction, Jong-Nam, disoriented and highly confused, staggered over to the information kiosk, but before he could attempt to sputter out what had just happened, he began to go limp and blind. He was soon wheeled off on a stretcher, but he flat-lined before he could make it to the hospital. The handkerchief, later recovered, tested positive for a lethal military-grade chemical weapon known as "VX."

Malaysian authorities had the women in custody just three days later: Siti Aisyah, from Indonesia, and Doan Thi Huong, a native of Vietnam. The duo, said to be in their late 20s, told cynical authorities how they had been fooled into believing that they were part of a prank show. The only detail that they could spare was the $90 paid to them by two anonymous men who were either Japanese or Korean.

It appeared to be an open-and-shut case, one that was almost certainly tied to Kim Jong-un and his regime. Authorities recalled how Huong had bolted straight into the bathroom following the attack to rinse off her hands, suggesting that she was worried about the VX seeping into her skin. Even more convincing, the scheme stunk of a traditional North Korean assassination plot. Back in 2011, state agents had taken on a similar attempt with a poison needle concealed inside a pen.

Whatever the case, the women, clearly caught on tape for the murder of Kim Jong-Nam, were tossed behind bars. 9 more individuals were later charged as accessories to murder – 1 Malaysian and 8 North Korean natives, among them a scientist who had resided in Kuala Lumpur for over a year. "The tragedy is that he really just wanted to be left alone," Jennifer Lind, a professor at Dartmouth College, remarked. "But because of his blood, and his birth, he couldn't be."

It certainly does not seem as if Kim Jong-un is going to change any time soon. The impending threat of war from North Korea continues. On July 4, 2017, the Supreme Commander celebrated America's Independence Day by launching an intercontinental ballistic missile for the first time in history, calling it a "gift to the American bastards." A little over a month later, citizens on the northern Hokkaido island awoke to the sound of ear-splitting missile sirens, warning of a missile soaring over Japan. It later fizzled out and disintegrated into three pieces as it plunged into the sea.

Whether or not these false alarms will ever cross the line into reality is a fate still unknown. As the old saying goes, only time will tell.

Online Resources

Other books about North Korea on Amazon

Bibliography

L Szoldra, P., & Bondarenko, V. (2017, April 18). How North Korean leader Kim Jong Un, 33, became one of the world's scariest dictators. Retrieved September 6, 2017, from http://www.businessinsider.com/kim-jong-un-life-2016-9/#kim-jong-un-has-a-theme-song-known-as-footsteps-6

Sang-Hun, C., & Sanger, D. E. (2011, December 19). Kim Jong-il, North Korean Dictator, Dies. Retrieved September 6, 2017, from http://www.nytimes.com/2011/12/19/world/asia/kim-jong-il-is-dead.html?pagewanted=all

Editors, D. M. (2011, December 29). 'The people are crying tears of blood': Millions of wailing North Koreans line snow bound streets in display of state-controlled grief for Kim Jong Il's funeral. Retrieved September 6, 2017, from http://www.dailymail.co.uk/news/article-2079237/Kim-Kim Jong-il-funeral-Millions-crying-North-Koreans-line-Pyongyangs-snow-bound-streets.html

Editors, D. M. (2012, January 13). Punished for not crying: Thousands of North Koreans face labour camps for not being upset enough about death of Kim Jong-il. Retrieved September 6, 2017, from http://www.dailymail.co.uk/news/article-2085636/North-Koreans-face-labour-camps-upset-death-Kim-Kim Jong-il.html

Szorlda, P., & Lubin, G. (2013, April 13). How a shy boy from North Korea became the world's scariest dictator*. Retrieved September 6, 2017, from http://www.thejournal.ie/kim-jong-un-childhood-864902-Apr2013/

Brooke, J. (2004, August 27). A Mystery About a Mistress in North Korea. Retrieved September 6, 2017, from http://www.nytimes.com/2004/08/27/world/a-mystery-about-a-mistress-in-north-korea.html

Glionna, J. M. (2011, December 24). Many women were linked to Kim Jong Il, but few had any influence. Retrieved September 6, 2017, from http://articles.latimes.com/2011/dec/24/world/la-fg-north-korea-women-20111225

Editors, B. (2017, April 27). Kim Jong-un. Retrieved September 6, 2017, from https://www.biography.com/people/kim-jong-un-21125351

Childress, S. (2014, January 14). What was Kim Jong-un Like as a Boy? Retrieved September 6, 2017, from http://www.pbs.org/wgbh/frontline/article/what-was-kim-jong-un-like-as-a-boy/

Editors, A. A. (2014, February 23). Kim Jong-un's childhood of 'Big Macs and pleasure girls' revealed. Retrieved September 6, 2017, from http://english.alarabiya.net/en/variety/2014/02/23/Kim-John-Un-s-childhood-of-Big-Macs-and-pleasure-girls-revealed.html

Fitfield, A. (2016, January 8). Asia & Pacific What do we know about Kim Jong Un? Very little. That makes this guy an expert. Retrieved September 6, 2017, from https://www.washingtonpost.com/world/asia_pacific/what-do-we-know-about-kim-jong-un-very-little-that-makes-this-guy-an-expert/2016/01/08/6fde1b98-b3bd-11e5-8abc-d09392edc612_story.html?utm_term=.3550823c6543

Austin, S. (2017, April 12). 10 Things You Didn't Know About Kim Jong Un. Retrieved September 6, 2017, from https://www.usnews.com/news/world/articles/2017-04-12/10-things-you-didnt-know-about-kim-jong-un

Levine, D. S. (2017, August 8). Kim Jong Un's Education: 5 Fast Facts You Need to Know. Retrieved September 6, 2017, from http://heavy.com/news/2017/08/kim-jong-un-education-age-switzerland-degrees/

Corbin, C. (2017, June 28). Family of David Sneddon, missing US student, says North Korea kidnapped him. Retrieved September 6, 2017, from http://www.foxnews.com/world/2017/06/28/family-david-sneddon-missing-us-student-says-north-korea-kidnapped-him.html

Power, J., Ozawa, M., & Macfarlan, T. (2015, June 5). Gorging on steak, cheese and two bottles of Cristal champagne in one sitting: Former chef reveals the extravagant tastes of Kim Jong-un that has led to North Korean dictator's massive weight gain. Retrieved September 6, 2017, from http://www.dailymail.co.uk/news/article-3112019/Former-chef-reveals-extravagant-tastes-Kim-Jong-led-North-Korean-dictator-s-massive-weight-gain.html

Editors, E. (2014, February 23). Vodka binges, secret smoking and Big Macs - the life of Kim Jong-un as a boy. Retrieved September 6, 2017, from http://www.express.co.uk/news/world/461408/Dictator-Kim-Kim Jong-un-used-to-binge-on-vodka-and-Big-Macs

Choe, S. H., & Fackler, M. (2009, June 14). North Korea's Heir Apparent Remains a Mystery. Retrieved September 6, 2017, from http://www.nytimes.com/2009/06/15/world/asia/15kim.html

Branigan, T. (2009, July 13). Kim Jong-il 'has pancreatic cancer'. Retrieved September 6, 2017, from https://www.theguardian.com/world/2009/jul/13/kim-jong-il-cancer

Bennett, D. (2011, December 20). Kim Jong-un Makes First Appearance as Kim Jong-il's Body Goes on Display. Retrieved September 7, 2017, from https://www.theatlantic.com/international/archive/2011/12/kim-jong-un-makes-first-appearance-kim-jong-ils-body-goes-display/334077/

Szoldra, P., & Bondarenko, V. (2017, April 18). How North Korean leader Kim Jong Un, 33, became one of the world's scariest dictators. Retrieved September 7, 2017, from http://www.businessinsider.com/kim-jong-un-life-2016-9/#kim-jong-un-was-born-on-january-8-1982-1983-or-1984-1

Fujimoto, K. (2004, Jan. & feb.). I Was Kim Jong Il's Cook. Retrieved September 7, 2017, from https://www.theatlantic.com/magazine/archive/2004/01/i-was-kim-jong-ils-cook/308837/

Editors, L. M. (2017, February 9). A world of difference. Retrieved September 7, 2017, from https://www.lovemoney.com/galleryextended/62439/kim-jong-uns-secret-life-of-luxury-while-his-people-struggle-to-survive?page=5

Editors, S. (2017, February 15). Jong-nam fell out of favour after fake passport episode. Retrieved September 7, 2017, from http://www.thestar.com.my/news/nation/2017/02/15/rise-fall-and-death-of-playboy-heirapparent-jongnam-fell-out-of-favour-after-fake-passport-episode/

Anderson, C. C. (2013, September 5). Chinese Internet Users Say This Completely Innocuous Video Is The 'Sex Tape' That Got Kim Jong-un's Ex Killed. Retrieved September 7, 2017, from http://www.businessinsider.com/hyon-song-wol-pornographic-video-kim-jong-un-ex-girlfriend-2013-9

Editors, K. J. (2012, July 9). Is Hyon the new first lady of NK? Retrieved September 7, 2017, from http://koreajoongangdaily.joins.com/news/article/article.aspx?aid=2955828

Editors, W. (2017, August 31). Hyon Song-wol. Retrieved September 7, 2017, from https://en.wikipedia.org/wiki/Hyon_Song-wol#Marriage_and_rumors_of_involvement_with_Kim_Kim Jong-un

Editors, A. N. (2017, July 2). North Korea: 4 facts about Kim Jong-un's rarely seen wife Ri Sol-Ju. Retrieved September 7, 2017, from http://newsable.asianetnews.tv/life/4-facts-about-north-koreas-kim-jong-un-rarely-seen-wife-ri-sol-ju

Castro, D. (2017, August 22). Ri Sol-ju, Kim Jong-un's Wife: 5 Fast Facts You Need to Know. Retrieved September 7, 2017, from http://heavy.com/news/2017/08/kim-jong-un-wife-ri-sol-ju-music-bio-missing-children-photos/

France-Presse, A. (2017, August 29). Kim Jong-un 'has fathered his third child' after wife disappeared from public eye. Retrieved September 7, 2017, from http://www.telegraph.co.uk/news/2017/08/29/kim-jong-un-has-fathered-third-child-wife-disappeared-public/

McDonald, M. (2010, October 9). Kim Jong-il's Heir Attends Parade. Retrieved September 7, 2017, from http://www.nytimes.com/2010/10/10/world/asia/10korea.html

DeFraia, D. (2012, July 18). North Korea: Kim Jong-un gets a promotion. Retrieved September 7, 2017, from https://www.pri.org/stories/2012-07-18/north-korea-kim-jong-un-gets-promotion

Editors, W. (2017, June 4). Footsteps (Ri Jong-o song). Retrieved September 7, 2017, from https://en.wikipedia.org/wiki/Footsteps_(Ri_Jong-o_song)

Branigan, T. (2012, July 6). North Korea's Kim Jong-un gets new official theme song. Retrieved September 7, 2017, from https://www.theguardian.com/world/2012/jul/06/north-korea-kim-jong-un-song

Williams, M. (2012, April 18). English transcript of Kim Jong Un's speech. Retrieved September 7, 2017, from http://www.northkoreatech.org/2012/04/18/english-transcript-of-kim-jong-uns-speech/

Choe, S. (2012, April 15). North Korean Leader Stresses Need for Strong Military. Retrieved September 7, 2017, from http://www.nytimes.com/2012/04/16/world/asia/kim-jong-un-north-korean-leader-talks-of-military-superiority-in-first-public-speech.html

Editors, E. (2017, June 8). How Kim Jong Un builds his personality cult. Retrieved September 7, 2017, from https://www.economist.com/news/asia/21723148-it-helps-be-grandson-god-king-how-kim-jong-un-builds-his-personality-cult

Ryall, J. (2013, May 16). Kim Jong-un had 'secret' daughter in 2010. Retrieved September 7, 2017, from http://www.telegraph.co.uk/news/worldnews/asia/northkorea/10060840/Kim-Kim Jong-un-had-secret-daughter-in-2010.html

Sherwell, P. (2012, April 7). North Korea promotes nuclear and missile chiefs as Kim Jong-un consolidates power before rocket launch. Retrieved September 8, 2017, from http://www.telegraph.co.uk/news/worldnews/asia/northkorea/9191814/North-Korea-promotes-nuclear-and-missile-chiefs-as-Kim-Kim Jong-un-consolidates-power-before-rocket-launch.html

Editors, B. (2012, April 13). North Korea rocket launch fails. Retrieved September 8, 2017, from http://www.bbc.com/news/world-asia-17698438

Cabinet of the DPRK. (2014). Retrieved September 8, 2017, from https://static1.squarespace.com/static/573c756e859fd06a1f830223/t/575a507ae32140bd67b97193/1465536634829/DPRK-Cabinet-Background-Guide.pdf

Choe, S. (2017, April 30). As Economy Grows, North Korea's Grip on Society Is Tested. Retrieved September 8, 2017, from https://www.nytimes.com/2017/04/30/world/asia/north-korea-economy-marketplace.html

Lankov, A. (2015, October 7). Kim Jong-un's recipe for success: private enterprise and public executions. Retrieved September 8, 2017, from https://www.theguardian.com/world/2015/oct/07/north-korea-recipe-for-success-economic-liberalisation-public-executions

Shim, E. (2015, July 8). Kim Jong Un is paranoid about food safety, says source. Retrieved September 8, 2017, from https://www.upi.com/Top_News/World-News/2015/07/08/Kim-Kim Jong-un-is-paranoid-about-food-safety-says-source/8121436368705/

Kim, T. (2014, December 23). Look At How Bizarre North Korea's 'Internet' Is. Retrieved September 8, 2017, from http://www.businessinsider.com/a-look-at-north-koreas-tightly-controlled-internet-services-2014-12

Fenton, S. (2016, June 9). Kim Jong-un claims to have cured Aids, Ebola and cancer with single miracle drug. Retrieved September 8, 2017, from http://www.independent.co.uk/news/world/asia/kim-jong-un-claims-to-have-cured-aids-ebola-and-cancer-with-single-miracle-drug-10332386.html#gallery

Cain, A. (2017, June 25). A look inside the daily life of Kim Jong Un, the North Korean dictator who's as secretive as he is dangerous. Retrieved September 8, 2017, from http://www.businessinsider.com/kim-jong-un-daily-life-2017-6/#over-the-years-kim-jong-un-has-continued-to-enjoy-a-pampered-existence-despite-international-sanctions-as-cnn-recently-reported-much-of-his-personal-piggy-bank-flows-from-illegal-activity-like-drug-and-weapons-sales-cash-counterfeiting-and-hacking-banks-10

Kim, S. (2015, August 27). Inside the luxury world of Kim Jong-un. Retrieved September 8, 2017, from http://www.telegraph.co.uk/travel/destinations/asia/north-korea/articles/Inside-the-luxury-world-of-Kim-Kim Jong-un/

Pleasance, C. (2017, April 21). Dictator's paradise: The secret retreat with 200ft pool yacht, waterslides and theme park rides where Kim Jong-un parties 'like it's Ibiza'. Retrieved September 8, 2017, from http://www.dailymail.co.uk/news/article-4433150/Secret-retreat-Kim-Jong-parties-North-Korea.html

Walker, T. (2014, December 17). The Interview: Sony Pictures cancels release of Kim Jong-un assassination film as intelligence officials link cyber-attacks to North Korea. Retrieved September 8, 2017, from http://www.independent.co.uk/arts-entertainment/films/news/sony-pictures-cancels-christmas-release-of-north-korea-comedy-the-interview-9932100.html

Greenwood, C. (2014, December 26). The Interview download: Comedy becomes best-selling and most pirated film on Christmas Day. Retrieved September 8, 2017, from http://www.mirror.co.uk/tv/tv-news/interview-download-comedy-becomes-best-selling-4877627

Lankov, A. (2014, June 11). Why Pyongyang's restaurant scene is thriving. Retrieved September 8, 2017, from https://www.theguardian.com/world/2014/jun/11/north-korea-pyongyang-restaurant

Editors, W. (2017, August 9). Ryongsong Residence. Retrieved September 9, 2017, from https://en.wikipedia.org/wiki/Ryongsong_Residence

Zinser, L. (2013, February 28). Rodman Meets With North Korean Leader, Courtside. Retrieved September 9, 2017, from http://www.nytimes.com/2013/03/01/sports/basketball/dennis-rodman-meets-north-korean-leader.html

Editors, I. (2016, December 27). Kim Jong-un bans Christmas, forces people to worship his grandma. Retrieved September 9, 2017, from http://newsinfo.inquirer.net/857154/kim-jong-un-bans-christmas-in-north-korea-forces-people-to-worship-his-grandma

Editors, T. (2016, May 9). North Korea, Always Quotable: 9 Memorable Statements From Kim Jong-un's Reign. Retrieved September 9, 2017, from https://www.nytimes.com/interactive/2016/world/asia/north-korea-kim-jong-un.html

Mansourov, A., PhD. (2014, December 16). Kim Jong Un's Nuclear Doctrine and Strategy: What Everyone Needs to Know. Retrieved September 9, 2017, from https://nautilus.org/napsnet/napsnet-special-reports/kim-jong-uns-nuclear-doctrine-and-strategy-what-everyone-needs-to-know/

Fitfield, A. (2017, September 5). For Kim Jong Un, nuclear weapons are a security blanket. And he wants to keep it. Retrieved September 9, 2017, from https://www.washingtonpost.com/world/asia_pacific/for-kim-jong-un-nuclear-weapons-are-a-security-blanket-and-he-wants-to-keep-it/2017/09/05/d7b7ecb8-9236-11e7-b9bc-b2f7903bab0d_story.html?utm_term=.ff855395e26c

Silva, C. (2017, March 23). NORTH KOREA'S KIM JONG UN IS STARVING HIS PEOPLE TO PAY FOR NUCLEAR WEAPONS. Retrieved September 9, 2017, from http://www.newsweek.com/north-koreas-kim-jong-un-starving-his-people-pay-nuclear-weapons-573015

Branigan, T. (2013, December 13). North Korea executes Kim Jong-un's uncle as 'traitor'. Retrieved September 9, 2017, from https://www.theguardian.com/world/2013/dec/13/north-korea-executes-kim-jong-un-uncle-jang-song-thaek

France-Presse, A. (2014, May 17). North Korean singer rumoured to have been executed appears on TV. Retrieved September 9, 2017, from https://www.theguardian.com/world/2014/may/17/north-korean-singer-rumoured-executed-appears-tv

Campbell, C. (2017, March 2). The Mysterious Death and Life of Kim Jong Nam. Retrieved September 9, 2017, from http://time.com/4688208/kim-jong-nam-north-korea-kuala-lumpur/

Wools, D. (2017, July 5). Kim Jong Un: Missile launch a 4th of July 'gift to American bastards'. Retrieved September 9, 2017, from https://www.timesofisrael.com/kim-jong-un-missile-launch-a-july-4-gift-to-american-bastards/

Henderson, B., Ryall, J., & Connor, N. (2017, August 29). 'All options are on the table': Donald Drumpf says world has received North Korea's message 'loud and clear' after Kim Jong-un fires missile over Japan. Retrieved September 9, 2017, from http://www.telegraph.co.uk/news/2017/08/28/north-korea-fires-missile-japan-warns-citizens-take-precautions/

Jones, J. (Writer). (2014, January 14). Secret State of North Korea [Television series episode]. In *Frontline*. Hardcash Productions.

Free Books by Charles River Editors

We have brand new titles available for free most days of the week. To see which of our titles are currently free, click on this link.

Discounted Books by Charles River Editors

We have titles at a discount price of just 99 cents everyday. To see which of our titles are currently 99 cents, click on this link.

12/18

98914915R00024

Made in the USA
Middletown, DE
10 November 2018